WASTOID: SONNETS

Wastoid
© 2014 Mathias Svalina

Published by Big Lucks Books
Washington, DC
BigLucks.com

ISBN: 978-1-941985-90-8

Cover art by Sara Woods

Titles set in OFL Sorts Mill Goudy
Text set in Crimson

First edition, November 2014

Wastoid

Mathias Svalina

BIG LUCKS BOOKS 2014

for Joshua Marie Wilkinson

WASTOID

The first time I met my lover he was a praying mantis. He extended one long green leg toward me & offered me his ipod. The headphones were two tiny preying mantises affixed to black wires. I inserted them into my ears & heard a sound I could not identify. It sounded like two wet bones rubbing against each other, but also like lakewater lapping off a handful of wet hair. Then I understood the sound. I was inside my lover's heart & the sound was his blood, how a glass of cold water on a hot day undoes itself. When I opened my eyes the recognizable world was gone & my lover was there: preying mantis body, preying mantis eyes, preying mantis mandibles biting through my preying mantis skin, eating my preying mantis eyes, understanding in the manner of a joystick.

WASTOID

My lover's brothers are hawks & his fathers are hawks. Before he could learn to kill he had to learn to fly, to glide & bank sharply & descend upon a rabbit, only then ripping its throat, ripping its throat out while the rabbit was still unaware. One night walking through the empty streets of Lagos my lover changed his murderous ways. He came across a jar in the middle of the sidewalk, a jar full of ball bearings. He dropped the ball bearings on a glass table & listened to each ball bounce with a unique ping.

WASTOID

A man possesses two things: his death & other men. A man must immerse himself in one or the other but never both. To immerse oneself in death is to become a shower curtain, a sleeve of red plastic cups tossed into the shopping cart beside the 12-pack of Hawaiian Punch in cans. To immerse oneself in another man is to become a contraption. There are so many men immersed in every man, to count them all would be flint, while edits scum last night's red plastic cups. The only choice is substance vs. form—both tame the unrammable will.

Wastoid

Youth is immortal. Take this streetlamp here, to my left. Let it serve as a cenotaph for youth. Though the boys who walk in its light be dead, servants will continue to replace its bulbs & weed-whack the weeds at its base. The servants will wear matching jumpsuits. They will speak in a series of beeps & whistles. After everyone who will have ever been young is dead, the servants of youth will continue. It is easy to see I am correct in this prediction, but also I am wrong about that other thing.

WASTOID

My lover makes lamps. He sees an old Chevy & turns it into a lamp. He watches Orion's Belt slide through the sky & turns it into a lamp. He sees the exposed wrist bones of a surgery patient & makes of them a lamp. He has written textbooks on lamp & swam in an ocean of lamp. He has transformed a runaway train into a lamp & watched as his lamps grew up, left home & became their own motives. You can always tell where my lover has walked by the burning trail of lamps. Each lamp burns all day & all night but even during the daytime it is dark here.

WASTOID

I first saw my lover in Sunken Gardens as the sun rose over downtown & we opened a warm bottle of champagne. Out of the bottle flew jewel-like flies, each carrying a tiny chandelier, each chandelier more beautiful than the last, beautiful in complexity & artistry & made more beautiful by diminution. I grew up in a house of doors. Mythic creatures like Jimmy Superfly Snukka & Lionel Richie could open any door, but I had to wait until a door was opened for me. Now I carry dozens of doors on my back wherever I go. My lover is walking down the street, his cellphone visible in the back pocket of his jeans, but with these doors on my back I'm behind too many doors. It's like I am my lover's imaginary friend, except I'm real.

WASTOID

My lover is a bronze statue of a deer. You purchased him at a garage sale. You & my lover are now in love. You love my lover because you know I love my lover & you love my lover in all the ways I taught you about love. But there is a sack of millet on your living room floor. And there is a hole in the corner of the sack of millet & mice approach the sack of millet & stuff their mouths with millet & run back to their hole beneath the refrigerator. You place the bronze statue of a deer on the mantel. You place beside it a vanilla scented candle & light that with a wooden match. You watch the mice run from the sack of millet to the refrigerator, trying to determine which mouse is me.

WASTOID

A young man looks in a mirror & it is the time to beget a child. There is no man, after all, who is more outstanding than a mirror. When the man kisses the mirror the mirror kisses the man & he gets a bit of mirror stuck to his lips. All through the day the world reflects itself, embeds itself, in his lips. There are fathers in the world & there are sons & there is not much else for the mirror, for the mirror is as hungry as the young man's mouth. No one remembers anyone as well.

WASTOID

My lover is an obstacle. Many think I must overcome him but I do not want to overcome him. I don't remember my dreams, but once I was in the ocean & it was blue like what a bomb feels & above me two whales swam lazily & I could see how each muscle worked in their bigness & their singing was the biggest door creaking on the biggest rusty hinges & also the biggest & most beautiful boy sighing the biggest sighs of receipt. I think this is why I like the universe & books & roots & computers & mountains & riots & love & the-river-after-it-rains: I don't go much for beauty without condition—everything impossible is part of me. My obstacles are true commas.

Wastoid

To lovers loving is simply work—hard, yes, but intentionally
so. All the while the boys' feet have grown roots that entangle
beneath the county fairgrounds. A love-act is a counterfeit
three-dollar bill. And all the boys & their wrinkling jowls
snatch at a gelatinous pit lake.

WASTOID

My lover has a father, a father, a father, a father, a father, a father, a father, a father, a father, a father, a father, a father, a father, a father, a father, a father, a father & a father. Often he opens the stomachs of enormous sharks & mackerel, squid & detritus spill onto the dock in a sloppy foam of gross shark-stomach juice. His fathers take photos of him beside each hanging shark & upload them onto twenty Facebook walls. Like a pipe, my lover's work is never done. There are so many sharks still living. I am an enormous shark. All day I eat messages in bottles. Occasionally, I find one written by my lover's fathers. *Dear son*, it reads, *Say 'unchanging.' Now say 'again unchanging.' The void is unchanging.* I wait for my lover to reel me in, hang me up, slide his thin knife into my underbelly & pull me open to find his way home to all my messages.

WASTOID

My lover is the sound of cars driving in the rain that I hear through my bedroom window. I had never truly heard this sound until I listened to that Elliot Smith song in which he sings *Street's wet you can tell by the sound of the cars*. And every time I drive by Omaha I think of that Moby Grape song "Omaha," which doesn't say the word Omaha & I wonder what *is* Omaha. On Google, I checked, there are about 267,000 hits for "dumb & dumber fan fiction erotica" but there are no hits for "sound of cars driving in the rain erotica." I don't know much about politics. I've never cared what gets found in the attics of old houses. But some things are going to change around here.

WASTOID

On the morning of his wedding the groom watched his betrothed walk their dog past their house & he considered his feelings for him. Thinking tends to clarify thoughts. He sat down at his desk to write his vows. He tapped his pencil to his teeth. Then chewed on the pencil's end. Then opened the big drawer & produced a blue pen. Finally he set his face determinedly, as if he were preparing to knock down a wasps' nest, & set the pen to the paper. He wrote the letter *L* & then crossed it out. He wrote a series of loops but it formed no recognizable letters. He wrote the word *SWARM* in his best handwriting. He stopped. He had never truly looked at *SWARM* before. Never this silently. He held the paper to his face & kissed the word until his spit smeared the ink & his lips were blue. He wrote the word again, beneath the soaked part of the paper, & again kissed it with all his competence.

WASTOID

My lover is a laugh track. He pours hot sauce on his eggs &
it is laughter pouring hot sauce on the eggs. He drives up
to the bank to deposit some checks & the car plumps with
laughing. On the street people hear him coming & they want
to laugh along. They search the street for something funny
& they always find it. At home I try to tell him the thing
that is wrong with me. The thing that is wrong with me is
shaped like a knife with two blades & it is stuck somewhere
between my lungs. But all the while there is the laughing &
after that more laughing, & one laugh, distinctive from the
rest, repeats its shrill staccato *Hoo-Hoo-Hoo*.

WASTOID

My lover has an enormous name. It only just fits in the minivan when we go to Home Depot. We used to fold the name up neatly for travel when our relationship was new & he wore all the jewelry that were gifts from me. But now my lover's name has such strength & such wealth that it is impossible to fold. There are so many things that command the attention of men—for instance, I love prizes. But my lover looks at photographs of horses online & looks at how much they cost & imagines what it would feel like to purchase a horse. He drags his name from one room to the next & rarely can I edge my way past it.

WASTOID

My lover has been stung by every insect on the planet. The worst sting, he claims, is from a common wooden rocking horse. I am a common wooden rocking horse. I have no idea where my stinger is & I am too apprehensive to ask my lover as it may remind him of the fact that I could sting him again. Each person, place, or thing has an insect sting but it is not always clear where the sting is located. And worse, the sting may disembowel you, so you have to be wary: you have to pause before you spend all night in the sculpture garden with the man you just met at the bar, before you bike to the middle of Wilderness Park & have sex on the bank of the dry Salt Creek. My lover claims that the clean, sparkling pain of my sting lingers for twelve hours, but we all know it is almost impossible to remember what it feels like to be sung to.

Wastoid

The horribles fall in love with people nobody sees. The people nobody sees wear thin shoes to leave small impressions on the dirt. They collect bottles in which they store their own skulls. On the horrible website where horribles discuss horrible things, the horribles discuss love & the finer things, new chef here, new virus there, a frilly skirt, a skilled flirt. When horribles arrive at the hotel their room is not booked. When they call the office no one has ever heard of them. The people nobody sees carry their purposes wherever they go. When a person nobody sees sees a horrible approach, one can see them stop, consider turning away, & then decide to continue forward, prepared to say hello to the horrible.

WASTOID

Once I was in love with four-leaf clovers, by which I mean I was in love with concept. My high school had this hill on which each other clover was four-leafed. It got to where four-leaf clovers were merely form. But four-leaf clovers were still interesting everywhere not this hill. I found myself within a steel house with no doors. There was the sound of water burbling, that steel smell that reminds me of old roads. And then I'd remove my hands from my pockets & they were covered with fresh young four-leaf clovers growing out of each pore, little uncurling leaves, roots, skin.

Wastoid

Every dollar bill bears the same beautiful child. Every time a dollar bill is touched it gives birth to itself, though the father be shameful or a sandbox full of bright plastic trucks. It is fear that makes the world so solid.

WASTOID

There are two moons, each in love with the other, but they orbit at opposite points of the same path. One moon, as a child, had an English Setter. For his father's funeral this moon wore a new black suit, but the English Setter jumped all over him until the black suit was covered with long white hairs & the young moon found himself, instead of being saddened, laughing & he rolled on the carpet with the dog, who was full of whatever it is in dogs that we call love. The other moon had never believed in anything until he saw the young moon rolling on the rug with his dog in his black suit covered in white hairs. Because the two moons cannot see one another they leave notes: *I saw a tree & it reminded me of you; I heard Glenn Gould's 1982 recording of* The Goldberg Variations *& I thought of you; you are with me in the ever-night.* Down on earth a father left his son in the car with the windows shut in the Home Depot parking lot.

WASTOID

My lover tries to tip the man in the tollbooth but the man in the tollbooth is a grandfather clock. The setting sun withers the flowers away & my lover collects each dried petal in a tiny glass vial. The grandfather clock in the tollbooth has stopped ticking & begun a long, low groan. Every noise is made against a backdrop of noise. Death is irrelevant: each car passes the tollbooth & leaves its dollar on the scratched steel shelf.

WASTOID

My lover is a drag race that starts on a city road & then moves to a gravel road & then ends tragically as one car plunges off the wooden bridge into the flooded river, black with mud. He contains the bliss of elation & the bliss of misfortune. But it takes more than intellect to never return. I don't hate my occupation, the furniture dead hands made, glasses dead mouths once lipped. The goal of art is to hold the drive-through window up to the world & it attends to me incessantly. When the boy who survived the car's plunge into the river crawled out onto the riverbank he couldn't remember a thing & everyone sincerely thanked him for this.

WASTOID

My lover is what is visible through the open window at night. Our love is what we love beyond the creek of snakes, where grass sprouts through the abandoned floorboards. Everything else is a box, a blocked drain. Inside is memory, outside is sweat. I am only my skin. I have filled my skin with pillows to make me look like I'm still here. The long grass gives my lover an air of fame. The night wind makes a blanket. My lover's inbetweenity is all of nature I want to know.

WASTOID

My lover is time. I take all my clocks apart to look for him. I look for him in the cracked & stained cathedral paintings. I look for him in the riverbanks & in the animals with webbed feet. The scariest thing in Stanley Kubrick's *The Shining* is not the axe breaking through the door, or the man in the bear suit, but how patterns repeat beyond what is watchable. I am permanently beautiful & young. I am uninspirable. I could write a good review of Jack Nicholson's character's novel.

WASTOID

The sun is so autonomous, so love-of-ruins. There are mountains down here & perfectly lovely meadows & some real nice streams, but the sun never cares. All the sun cares about is its emotions & how he looks when he has these emotions. The sun has a three-way mirror & he poses wearing one emotion & studies what it looks like from every angle. Then he poses wearing another emotion & does the same. The sun could do anything it wants but all it wants is to be seen demonstratively having emotions. But when it is cloudy, I wonder if the sun doesn't flatter those dark & deadpan clouds.

WASTOID

My lover is a wink. He's all stay-stay but also all slow-slow. We dance when he wants me to dance. And the reverse is also true, eyes aglow by party-lights. A man has so many shadows in the overlapping streetlights—he is a convergence of many shadows. I am incidence, the dream of already. But during the day I am wearing a blue wig with a page-boy haircut. I am taking photos of my outfits & posting them daily. We are dancing on the ceiling. We are gotta-gotta cut it loose. It's silly—it's common—but I don't mind stealing bread from the mouths of decadence.

WASTOID

The love dispensaries had a price war, pricing love lower &
lower until finally they would pay a customer to love, hand
out fresh love for free on the ped-mall. Resultantly, no one
wanted to love & things got wrinkly & damp. Those left who
would love spent restless nights alone in their apartments
lying on the couch then getting up to check email on their
desktop & then back to the couch. On TV men in expensive
clothes appeared on lavish sets & promised to befit one
another, studio lights glittering on all the smeared makeup.

WASTOID

When I was born my brother held me up to the men with cunts. They gave me an enormous roll of string & addressed it to *My Lover*. When he received it & found me we got to kissing. I am kissing my lover at a table on which sits one wine glass, a saltshaker & another saltshaker. My head is a mass of strings tied into knots. We will forever be kissing, forever at this table, forever forgetting there could be space between two things. There are things we believe, like men, & other men, & there are things we must believe to believe, like knots. Each morning my lover unties one of the knots that make my head & soon I know I will be left with only the drunk moon propped on the limbs of a skeletal oak & that's OK—I too revere the drunkenness of a swamp.

WASTOID

The men buried beneath my house are all named Neil. There is something in my room, in the corner of my room, behind the television. It has bendable arms & legs. When someone sees the thing in my room the thing in my room gets dirty & the Neils beneath the house bend their arms & legs this way & then that, shaking the house. What one Neil does all Neils do, until they are exhausted & glad to be done living & the Mayor gives a press conference. Then the Mayor drives his car home & parks his car in the driveway & when he opens the car door all of him, like spoiled milk, spills out of the car.

Wastoid

My lover tore me into three pieces. He kept one piece in a Kohls bag. One piece he sent into the ocean in a submarine & the submarine stayed at the ocean floor until it ran out of air & the crew used the piece of me to breathe. The third piece became a chef at a vegetarian restaurant. He uses so much tamari that his food is inedible, but it is the only vegetarian restaurant in town. A line of fresh stumps leads to his graveyard, to the plot where his grave has already been dug. Beside the grave, the gravedigger sits with his shovel in his hand. I do not mean the Gravedigger, the monster truck, I mean a guy named Steve.

WASTOID

My lover is fire & I am also fire. Though we have different fuels, we are the same feat, the same lean-into-the-void. When we get too close it is impossible to tell us apart.

WASTOID

Music swells & fades. The voiceover begins. My lover is wearing a fake beard & the clock strikes midnight. He burns a paper covered with strange symbols. May I suggest that self-love is wasted love, or is that the work of a lover? Regardless we know the devil is burning out there in the woods. He has enormous teeth & terrible claws & smoke surrounds him. Everyone can see him, every single person in the word, but they can only tell the story of seeing him once. Most tell the story immediately & then they have nothing left of their youth. My lover takes the story & buries it beneath the dirt & plants a birch tree over it. After it sprouts he carves his initials into the bark. His initials are YOUTH HOMICIDE.

WASTOID

My lover is the Fourth Crusade. He is always sacking the city. When I am in love with him I hear the screams of people being murdered, raped, destroyed in every way. They are terrible screams. They are very terrible screams. And what strikes me somehow as saddest is watching a crusader pull the heavy lead lining of a roof down & carry it back to Western Europe. I am neither a crusader nor a Constantinopolitan: I am watching what has to happen because history works like a shovel or like the seeds inside an apple. The bejeweled buildings burn & even this I am in love with. All these books are spread across my floor & I sometimes want to be able to feel the feeling of my blood pushing through my veins, to have all my nerves on the inside of my veins, to be the inside-out man.

WASTOID

Each day I put my hands inside the oven & search for my
lover. This is where intimacy stays when glistening is visible.
Youth is symbolized by the use of justice. Justice, in this use,
covers arguments in rotation. A symbol is a summary—
namely if youth is the son then the father must die outside,
in the trunk of the dogwood, his damages revving a cocktail
party of pain.

WASTOID

A man fell in love with a bomb. The bomb was strapped to another man's chest & the man grew jealous. The other man carried the bomb into a busy street & detonated it. Many people died & many cars were damaged. After the police left the scene the man went to the busy street & searched for pieces of the bomb. He was happy the other man was gone but unhappy that the bomb was no longer a bomb. He collected pieces of shrapnel that may have been from the bomb. He collected footage of the bomb exploding. He sat on his blue futon & watched the footage on repeat, stroking the sharp shrapnel until his fingers felt like sponges.

WASTOID

My lover is a quilt made of tinfoil. A full description of all the superior qualities of this quilt would make readers doubt that any quilt could have such extraordinary qualities. The writing on it is in perfect ancient Greek. It is a really great quilt. I am not exaggerating. I am stretching myself into two writers so that I can tell you more about this quilt. If the quilt ever has a boy I hope to be able to see my reflection in its shiny side, no matter how warped & crinkled I may look.

WASTOID

This poem says that time passes swiftly: *Time passes swiftly*.
But the difference between an ocean & its shore takes mere
minutes to understand & after that you have to understand it
for the rest of your life. When I walk outside to fetch the mail
there is a thick white cloud around my head & it obscures my
vision. I want the sun to make my skin feel tight & it will but
not quite. Then Death arrives with his big black cloak & his
scythe a'ready for reaping. We sit on my orange couch & I
give Death the bad seat, the one with broken springs.

WASTOID

If you see my lover on the street feel free to offer him a hot dog, though he may refuse. Feel free to offer him a slurpee, though he may refuse. Feel free to offer him a rolled up sheet of hand-made paper, a jar of sand, a gummy bear, a trombone, though any of these he may refuse. It's not that my lover does not want these things—it's that you are holding a document & every document is an emotion. To take from you the thing you are is not to hold your foot in the door, it is to recreate you.

WASTOID

My mirror keeps telling me to take out the trash. I have four bags of trash in my bedroom, one bag of trash in the bathroom & one bag of trash in the kitchen. I will never grow old while there is trash in my house & this upsets the mirror. The mirror is making crinkle-fries in the oven & I can smell fry-smell throughout the house. I look for the stairs that lead downstairs but all the stairs only lead upstairs. Upstairs thousands of thousands of men give bottles of milk to thousands of babies. The mirror tells me that there is so much trash it will soon be my heart that is unable to beat. This appears to be a warning. The windows will not close.

WASTOID

Whatever my lover looks at becomes a wish. For the wish to be fulfilled he steps inside of it & leaves a piece of himself in there. My lover has many triggers, lined up along his spine & arms. A wish walks up to him & chooses a trigger & then the wish pulls the trigger. If the wish has pulled the correct trigger the piece of my lover my lover has left within the wish explodes & the wish disappears & the weather changes & people win lotteries & other stuff happens. My lover is always looking at something & never at me.

WASTOID

A man has guests over for dinner but the man does not have his man over. The man's man lies in bed, picturing the man serving roasted asparagus & lamb. Then the man steps out of the man's man's picturings & sits down on a foldout chair beside the man's man's bed. There are many spies, so the two men must be careful. They must not allow love identity. There is a bit of irony to this, because two of the spies are in love & the first spy pried open the head of the second spy & left a handful of river stones therein. Meanwhile, in the man's house, his guests search the cabinets for mint jelly, but there is none to be found.

Wastoid

When my lover wears tight jeans you can see his man-penis pushed down the right side of his leg. It's not weird, now that everyone knows Buchenwald was built on a hill where Goethe once walked with Eckermann. I am the wind making a resonant hum through the power lines, which the most pretentious grad student makes his friends stop & appreciate when his friends only want to talk about who did what in what to what. I am what-has-already-been-done-once. I apply for jobs though there are no more jobs, no trees, no places for trees, only lonely droning laptops. Modern man walks through his day like an inside-out mirror, but everyone looks better in tight jeans, sometimes.

WASTOID

In this poem I am going to assume the persona of an old man reflected in a full-length mirror: I am a tree. I have leaves. In winter I have no leaves. Sometimes, in winter, where there were once leaves, thousands of dogs' tails grow out of my branches & wag. When I go to church the women want me to go get up on that altar & sing. Then the candles snuff out & it is nighttime in church. The wicks still glow red. You must love me, my congregation, because I am old & the red obliterates all other colors.

WASTOID

My lover moved into my eyes. He hired a moving company with a big white truck. They wrapped the antiques in blankets when they moved them into my eyes, so as not to scratch them. When my lover leaves my eyes each day to go to work, he locks them closed & I spend all day with my eyes shut, enjoying the sun on my face. When he comes home I watch him make dinner, pour himself a glass of wine & eat in front of the TV. He seems happy & I am happy for him, but the only furniture I own is my alarm clock.

WASTOID

When my lover is amorous, he is the American version of himself. When he is lusty, he is the Dutch version of himself. My lover makes sense because the Dutch version of him sits beside the American version of him. They share many interests: faces, water, enormity. They hold out their hands to each other & one slaps the other's hand & then the other slaps the other's hand & they smile so large it is like a smell. I am always wearing green. My voice hangs around my throat like a dead jay. When the American version of my lover & the Dutch version of my lover walk together, a van of high-school teachers slowly follows them with the lights off. The teachers wait for the best moment to strike. They are so eager to strike. On the radio in the van a familiar song plays. Is it the Scorpions? Is it Whitesnake? No. No. It is neither of those bands.

WASTOID

A man makes an offense of the law. The law leans down
& whispers a reproving whisper in the man's ear. Then the
law enters the man's ear. Then the law is something the man
hears, both an outside & physical act of his body. There is so
much law in a man—the word *sensual* only conveys half of it.
Half of the man is guilty & the other half of him is innocent,
but the quieter half is now walking away.

WASTOID

My lover is a trampoline. Nothing not already him becomes him. I grew up beside a burning house. The house would not stop burning, no matter how many trucks drove by. I lived like a canyon killing a praying man—things happened & I did not know how or why to do. The hundred-year woods behind the canyon, me inside the canyon, two dogs, breath escaping the cold's black pepper, boys jumping on the trampoline & that bundt-sound of boys on trampoline: you know that movie where nothing happens? I love that movie. I let the seasons decide the questions' only answer.

WASTOID

Moral particularism had a thing with a waffle iron. Often they sat on a park bench in a park at night making out. The waffle iron was never plugged in, but moral particularism loved to imagine it was plugged in & how his burnt tongue would stick to the metal. The waffle iron is happy when he is making waffles, but not at his happiest. He is happiest when looking, eating, & staying up until dawn, but he was not built for these things & they never feel as right as making waffles. Moral particularism could not decide if the fantasy of the burnt tongue could justify this thing with the waffle iron. Just then a truck carrying pharmaceuticals tipped over beside the park & millions of bottles of colorful pills spilled over the grass.

WASTOID

My lover is an echo. I must continue speaking to keep him alive. I follow my lover into the mountains & seek him out among the crags. I yell his name & he repeats his name & then he disappears. I worry that others may travel through the canyon, lost & thirsty & afraid, yelling out for help & their help returning to them through my lover. I worry that my lover will always be beyond my sight, regardless of my beauty, birth, wealth, & spite.

Wastoid

My physical senses do not love you. These skins only make a body, not love. Instead, the stone loves you. The stone maintains the house. The stone mortifies whoever can't define it, repeating itself in every direction, growing wide like a paraphrase. But in spite of my physical senses there are slaves in the world & men are raped each day. In this regard, the earth robs me of self-control. My only choice is stone like I do not blue. Nevertheless, I desire you bonfire.

WASTOID

I bought a writer's block from an antique store. It was very expensive because it was very old & had a lovely patina. My lover first set the writer's block in the guest room. Then he moved it to the living room. Then, suddenly, there were nine writer's blocks, one in each room. The house was infused with stifling. The problem is that I do not believe in God. So when God appeared, manifested in these nine writer's blocks, I tried to convince him he was a metaphor. But then God challenged me to find the original writer's block. I went from room to room, but all I could find was my lover, sitting at his desk, grading an unending stack of papers.

WASTOID

My lover is dead. At his funeral he gives his own eulogy. He says *Don't mourn me when there is so much suffering in the world. I will play with the worms as they eat my body. I am bringing all these bells into the grave with me.* Then my lover lies down in his casket. Someone has a jug & someone else has a washtub bass & just like that there is a jugband playing old-timey music. But as the musicians play their hands disintegrate into dust & so they play with their wrists. Then their wrists disintegrate into dust & so they play with their elbows. But they kept disintegrating until only their deaths are playing the music. The music is good, but someone behind me keeps talking on his cellphone & it kind of ruins the experience.

WASTOID

A man stole all the beauty. It was on his table in yellow & red plastic bottles when he ordered a burger & the assumption was that he would use some & leave the bottles on the table when he left but instead he stole all the beauty. At home, he hid the beauty in his hamper below a layer of dirty clothes. The cops arrived & searched his house, but when they opened the hamper they were like *Ew, dirty clothes*, & did not search it. With all the beauty stolen people had nothing traditional to love, so they began to love other things, like boats & receipts. The stars continued to shine & the trees grew pink & sweet each spring, but no one really gave a shit.

Wastoid

During their monthly meeting, the homeless men who appear in commercials for non-profit agencies all chew gum the color of raw whale. Each homeless man is in love with a man who attends a monthly meeting of cancer survivors in the room next door. If one could draw lines between the homeless actors & their beloved cancer survivors it would all be parallel lines. It would look like someone could write some very complicated music across the lines. It would look like many things dragged across a desert's sand. The cancer survivors are each waiting for their homeless man to make the first move, but the homeless men are unsure. They are in commercials, which is pretty cool, but they are also homeless, which makes things difficult.

WASTOID

I am in love with the mile. But the mile is in love with a groan. My beloved exists between any two points a mile apart. I mark his beginning & I love it, but with each step he begins again & I can only know him beginning. I keep walking until I groan, hoping I make the groan he is in love with but the groan my beloved is in love with is the groan so simultaneously hopeful & disillusioned that it can only be groaned by those who have studied long the ways of seed & thread. I manage the dog grooming shop behind the Bennigans, but I spend most of my day in the office looking at porn. In porn love is always demonstrated: one man comes on another man's face. One man comes on another man's face—it is like forgiveness & the photographer is the priest.

WASTOID

A dark shadow looms outside the window. Inside, I continue my day: I wash dishes, I adjust crooked paintings on the wall. When the doorbell rings, I stand quietly & don't move. The doorbell rings again & then finally the person at the door leaves. During the day it is difficult to see the dark shadow, but I always knows it's there. I remove my shirt & trousers in the bedroom. I lie down on my bed. I keep my socks on. By closing my eyes tightly I keep nostalgia at bay. The dark shadow jots some thoughts down in his moleskine. There is so much a dark shadow can never tell me. So much about it is unseeable. Like when you look at an enormous rock. How much of the rock is evident & how much of it is you?

WASTOID

My lover is the best part of a play. He dies while addressing
the audience, crumpling like a falling siege engine, his voice
both steadfast & rye. He doesn't even have to wear a fake
beard. He doesn't even have to use a machine. I am always
out there on the streets, in the malls, in the emergency
rooms, searching for the best chest to rip a t-shirt off of: a
paradox of two absences, two confidences. I'll cut my hair,
use an accent: I don't mind. I'll linger sweetly in the bridge to
each song. I love my lover but the show must go on.

WASTOID

A grave fell in love with a mirror. The grave had a bright future but the mirror did not. They took photos of themselves, camera at arm's length, squeezed cheek-to-cheek with smiles. They dropped wheels at the top of tall hills & watched them roll all the way down. They held hands in parks. But a mirror is a continuity & every time the grave looked in the mirror all he could see were stereotypical images of death. Every lover has at least one father & some of them have a certain month of the year during which everyone tells him how great he is. That's the good news. The bad news is that no grave can rest when there is work to be done.

WASTOID

My lover is the glow surrounding a glowing firefly. I am a
fire. Beside me my lover's glow is imperceptible. Above me
Mars spreads his red legs & slit-clouds slur the obese moon.
Whatever is lit by my lover is a pattern: a footprint, a fat
finger's whorls. We leave ourselves behind & what is left
dittos the self. *Now*, he says, his tone radiant. And then again
he says *Now.* I am in my house but there is no roof. I am like
the sun I am so dumb. The stars burn like splattered blood.
Everything is on fire. The remote control is in my hand but
the TV won't turn off.

WASTOID

Summer was in love with Spring. But then, on stage, Spring sang a song about Summer that angered him. It angered him so much he switched places with Fall to avoid Spring. The leaders of men were angry because the food would begin to grow in Spring & then immediately have to be harvested, not fully grown, in Fall. They proposed a trip to the beach where Summer lives to ask him to switch back with Fall. The leaders of men wanted to bring a dumptruck full of flowers because Summer likes flowers, but it took so long to collect the flowers it was Winter by the time they reached the beach. The leaders of men died & most of the men who were alive then died as well & there was blood & the other stuff over & over again until no one could remember a time in which Summer followed Spring. And all the while Spring had just been tidying his condo, finding old frames at garage sales & framing every thing he owned.

Wastoid

A lover persists long after death because every lover has many ears. Most lovers have ten ears, though some are only buds while the lover is alive & they bloom after the lover is dead. The ear is a symbol of change. In folktales when one finds an ear on the road one is suddenly holding a hand-written letter from Erasmus Darwin, one turns on the shower & a thousand ears spurt out. But tradition differs from practical investment: ten boys can find more vials of blood than six can. When the first ear blooms from the grave it is a happy occasion. But by the tenth the groundskeeper on the riding lawnmower doesn't even bother to swerve.

WASTOID

My lover is one day before a heart attack. He is feeling like a stack of books is on the chest, the left arm tingling & feeling heavy. Wherever my lover goes there goes discomfort & realization of mortality. When we meet at the mall, wait in line at the Au Bon Pain, the line dissipates before us. I am an ancient curse against Fistus, a Roman senator. *Crush, kill & crush Fistus the senator*, I read. *May Fistus dilute, languish, sink & may all his limbs dissolve*, I go on. I'm really quite unkind, but who is to say who dies by fate & who is crushed by magic? Some people get famous & some people walk out of rooms muttering to themselves. With all the new choices at the Au Bon Pain, it was tough to make up our minds. My lover got the Black Forest Ham with cheddar. I got the Black Angus Roast Beef with cheddar.

WASTOID

My lover has so much beauty that he must run away from the beauty or it will kill him. He spends his entire life in flight. He races away from me constantly & I founder in the murk of his trailing beauty. The beauty grows stronger at night & often I offer him a ride in my Firebird, letting him sleep as I race down back roads in the Shenandoah Valley. Sometimes people stand still on the escalator & my lover is too shy to push past them & the beauty catches up with him & his features fill with beauty until his skin drips from his face. Then he must scrape the beauty from his body & fling it all off to the stones. All the little oblivions & Caligulas may generate their limbs from stone, but beauty is used to a tombier nature.

WASTOID

I was in love like a hawk. But my lover was in love like Yoplait. I tried to love him like a library book but he said my love was like a grove. He claimed his love was a reciprocation but his love was the Body Shop at Fair Oaks Mall. I buried my love in a wooden box in the middle of the park & then the sprinklers came on & I was soaked. The next morning I found my love in the alley, crawling on two broken legs. It was so sad to see a creature so abject, such a code. His broken bones scraped audibly & when I finished the whole opened like a bandage.

WASTOID

My lover is a tomb. In that way he lives twice. Once as the tomb & once as the new-milk boy. As the tomb he is complete but silent as firm air. As the new-milk boy he speeds through suburban neighborhoods, dropping off bottles of new-milk before the sun tips over the mountains. In his wake praise clusters in catkins. The sun shines, yes, but the sun cannot be seen from the tomb. I am that false rage preceding the tomb, that legitimacy death gives to chandeliers. Where does desire drive us when one can only ask a child to conform?

WASTOID

A man gave birth to a ferris wheel. All night the ferris wheel would circle its axle, whispering beautiful things to itself in a language humans could not understand. The men swinging gently in the ferris wheel's arms only heard metal squeak against metal. When the ferris wheel's father died the ferris stood at the lectern at the funeral & described all the things that made his father great. After the funeral, the church hosted a potluck & relatives stood beside the ferris wheel eating macaroni salad & saying things like, *You still doing that carnival thing?* & *You look pale*, but when he responded they could not understand him. The ferris wheel understood this was the last time he would ever see these relatives & he was cool with that. Though his friends told him not to, that night the ferris wheel returned to his job at the carnival. The men stepped into his arms, the squeaking of metal on metal sounded like so many white plastic crosses.

WASTOID

My lover has never danced in public nor in private, despite this he is regarded as the greatest dancer in the world. It is the way he brushes his teeth, the way he sniffs at the wet wine cork, the way he signs off every email—business or private—with the exclamation *Cheers!* I am the man who was born with a snail shell. My snail shell did not grow very large & so it only protects a small portion of my back—I am unable to retract into it. While my lover goes through the day with perfect poise & acuity, I'm left feeling an unarticulatable discomfort with Jonathan Franzen's essays.

WASTOID

When I was a boy I stepped on a blackbird & then no one could speak. It was as though for a time I existed, as though I had a place in the world. All the lights were very bright inside the shopping center & the escalators ran all night. I touched my throat to feel for a pulse & my lover was there, how a dogwood tree is there for the bird. Outside in the parking lot stood a small man of disorder. He was not my lover & there was no my lover as far as I could see. And there was someone else there: a strange man with black eyes whom I could not dispel. I do feel that perhaps I'm trying to reach out for other things. Is this love, this walking through the black tunnel into another but different blackness?

WASTOID

My lover is a lightning-struck tree. Bits of his soft wood sit scattered across the lawn. The power is out & the neighborhood smells like ozone. My lover & I desire beauty & flowers & would love to buy a house, but a lightning-struck tree is only himself in the moment of the strike. After that he is a famine-self, awaiting hilarious chainsaws. It is not pity, my love. I hold a meaty piece of the shattered tree in my hand & it is damp & smooth to the touch. Yesterday someone drew chalk dick-&-balls on the sidewalk in orange chalk, but now, after the rainstorm, after the lightning & the strike, only a faint smudge of orange remains.

WASTOID

There is a man named Nature & another man named Naturer. They battle one another for so long that they realize they are in love & one cuts off the top of his body & the other one cuts off the bottom of his body & they become one person, leaving their other half for the beetles. Some poems attempt to explain things & how they relate to human life. Another example is how one can look at the moon & call it waxing or waning, but it's really not the moon—it is the animal clawing at the door with its cruel claws. But take heart, in time its cruel hands will sprout.

WASTOID

My lover has a bear's genitals. At a full sprint a bear is
much faster than a man & my lover is always sprinting—
therefore his bear genitals travel faster than his human body
& he is always in pursuit of them, always waxing repines
about harmony's hopelessness. I am the empty air between
my lover & his bear genitals. There is nothing to me. I am
disjunction's void, the interpretation's twitch. The first time
you fuck your lover is a doting time & best forgotten, but
some records begin with such memorable lines: *Back in the
day when I was a teenager; Jesus died for somebody's sins but not
mine; You can leave, but it's gunna cost you.*

WASTOID

An actor fell in love with a photograph of himself on the twenty-third page of a liberal arts college brochure. In the photograph the actor is acting doubtful, doubt showing in his doubting scowl. His suit has an out of date style, though the precise era is ambiguous. Blurry images of actors & crew lean into the background expectantly, willing the actor more & more recognizable doubt. In this photograph of himself the actor discovers the heart of acting: is he in love with himself? the photograph? the need for the stage? To answer these questions the actor opens his mouth & removes the cow's tongue wedged inside. One can fill one's mouth with any debris, one can catapult many venomous snakes into the ships of one's rivals, but a stage is raised above a floor.

WASTOID

My lover watches *CSI: Miami* twenty-four hours a day, waiting for David Caruso to remove his black sunglasses. While *CSI: Miami* plays there can be nothing wrong in the world. The whole world pauses to watch along, waiting for David Caruso to remove his black sunglasses. There is so much wrong in the world, so many throats cut for the cameras, so many houses built on sinners' bones, but my only hope is that my lover watches *CSI: Miami* forever. All the streets become one way, all the clouds are poisonous—I tug & I tug at my black sunglasses but my face refuses to release them.

WASTOID

My lover is *deus ex mechina*. To see him I attend shitty plays & wait until the end. I fantasize about him: I see a man immobile before a revolving door to a shopping mall, seemingly suddenly struck senseless by senselessness & I think of how if my lover was here an insurance agent could show up *out of the blue* & give the man a *fat check* from a *long-lost uncle*'s life policy. When the human cannonball finds his boyfriend in the arms of the world's shortest man, my lover allows them to all survive the earthquake. I am the nerves of the foot of a man in his twenties who lives in the middle of Rome—I must register the earth without making the mind aware of this earth—must allow the body to stay upright without willing it. Someday someone will survive me.

Wastoid

The dead organist in the refrigerator still plays for the congregation. He believes one should not live in isolation. He believes in the transformative power of art. The refrigerator's pipe organ was constructed in the same city where the man studied music—he feels with it an affinity that he could call love. When he plays the parishioners hear cold stillness, feel rigid limbs, the refrigerators' stained glass windows strain. What we do lasts in melody's muscle memory. What we love preserves in the cold dark. Love is love, a chain state, a score. But what chord? What pedal? What great cold welcomes human-to-human connection & thoroughness? Pain brings no one back. It brings him back each time.

WASTOID

My lover is imagery of military, winter, & commerce. He pastes himself in textbooks & picture books. He appears on CNN daily, though more frequently in winter. I am a sunflower among many sunflowers in a thick glass vase. The water we sit in once was fresh but now it smells so swamp. Barrenness encroaches on my swirled face. My stem has gone gummy. My lover thinks me narcissistic, but all I want is the fire that all deserve. I watch his explosions, his marches, his storms, but I am clad in the tatters of persistence. To refrain from imagery is to refrain from a devourable self. Each time my lover puts an old dollar bill in his wallet it emerges crisp & antiseptic. And always he is paying for things.

WASTOID

A novel fell in love with a science book. They were very far away from each other on the shelf, neither a book one reads again & again, or consults on sunny days.

WASTOID

A young man asked the sun to his prom. Unfortunately, the prom was at night. The sun was embarrassed because he can't go out at night & he turned the young man down without explanation. The young man was so sad he became a boy. The sadder he grew the younger he grew until he became an anole with a missing tail. The young man-anole ran up & down the elm trees, trying to get the sun's attention but the sun could not see him. The young man-anole gave himself new nicknames he thought the sun might find cool. He tried Noodle. He tried Ball. He tried Tremor. All the while the sun did not react. The young man-anole eventually grew up & got a job in middle management, never knowing that at night the sun stayed up late, watching old episodes of *Wonder Years* in bed on his laptop. He'd never seen *Wonder Years* before, so all the episodes were new to him.

WASTOID

My lover is unborn. He has nothing but names & impressions. All I really want to do is love everyone but sometimes in the recordings it is difficult to distinguish between me & the cello. My lover squeezes the breath out of me & replaces it with his breath. His breath is unborn & pure. I exhale fluid. I say words that have not yet developed meaning. Every body is a perfect untying. Every love is a burning cop car. There is too much of my lover in me.

WASTOID

A lover dies so many times that he cannot know he is dying or when he is no longer dead. My lover died & died & died & in the routine my grief grew recalcitrant. He would die & I would continue to pump bitter chemicals & milky white blood through his body. He would die & the body would float lazily on the hot night air. He died so often that I never knew when he was dead or not-dead. I made the sea stop splashing & held my ear to my lover's chest but there I heard three heartbeats. It's like those egg creams in New York or how insanity is not a medical term but a legal one.

WASTOID

My lover has grown another lover out of himself & now he has no need for me. When he looks at me it is as if he is looking at a curtain. Throughout the day I see many men—men walking dogs, men lying on the grass, men with hardhats—but I have never seen a man so unimpressed with a curtain. When my lover used to have a halo I ate only a tiny bit each night, though I wanted to eat it all at once. Over the years the halo grew smaller & smaller until I was biting the skin from my lover's head, trying to get the last bits of the halo, trying to find a chord. The new lover who grew out of my lover has a fresh halo, which my lover has begun to nibble—I can see the tooth marks. I see many things—chalk, bulldozers, guitar strings—& all of them are horrible.

WASTOID

My lover is a punch bowl. But love decays in the perfection each moment makes. In other words life is Trans Am, & you & I, merely Firebirds. In other words my lover rummages through packages of pantyhose, slips one into his briefcase & walks toward the revolving door. I am the counter on which the packages of pantyhose, in a basket, rest. And then I am the light refracting through the revolving door glass. There are no newspapers to flatten, no skin to graft onto a burnt leg. The host pours more vodka into the punchbowl. All the party guests dip the ladle in: the sweeter the punch the more vivid is forgetting. They are all my lover's lovers.

Wastoid

My lover is a single musical note but he only exists inside chords. I can never distinguish him from the notes he travels with, though he is the note that rings in my tinnitus ears, the note an empty propane tank makes banging against a stone wall. Music is a lot like youth in that a chord is tranquil but a single note needs a keycard. Every thing is symbolic of some other thing—that's why men hate art. But I drive these hills with the top down. Listen to this note: *la*. Now listen to this one: *la*. They are two different notes, yet each sounds like car exhaust.

WASTOID

I arrive each morning to the sun smiling that smile that's like, *Dude, seriously: jaeger-bombs.* And the sun says *Sup?* And I'm like, *You know.* And at Chatauqua there is a moon bounce with a snarling generator but no children, the park is empty but for me & the sun & what are we supposed to make of this? I think I named this life hair-of-the-dog. I think I like love how the pier likes the party on the tied-up yacht. And now the trees & grass of the park have disappeared & it is just dirt & the moon bounce & the generator & the sun & me. And then even the dirt is gone & the sun & I are suspended & the moon bounce & the generator are suspended & the generator's snarl sounds like blood. And now where is the sun & the moon bounce? It's just me & the generator & his voice & my voice sound like the same voice in this emptiness. One day all this will heal. I think I liked love better when he was a synonym for blood.

WASTOID

When I look in my mirror, Max Ernst looks back at me. I cannot make him speak, cannot make him smile. He looks at me disinterestedly, like starch, like brotherhood is sterile parallel lines birthing themselves an infinity. I smile & he only stares. I sing my favorite Prince song with all the screeches & screams & he stares. I evoke a flower's wilting stage & he climbs to the precarious top of a stepladder. My hair falls out & his hair falls out. I put the noose around my neck & he puts the noose around his neck. The pace of time or the loss of it breeds in each mirror's reflection. There are three more things for me to see in mirrors, but Max Ernst died on April first, nineteen seventy-six, of a heart attack, one day before his eighty-fifth birthday, back when I was eighty-five.

WASTOID

A soundbite loved a car stalled atop train tracks as the train approaches. *I'm so tired*, the stalled car said to the soundbite, *Too tired to stare at the ocean, too tired to wear a red turtleneck sweater.* The soundbite wanted to say so many things to the stalled car but it could only say the out of context sentence that it is, endlessly replicatable & reusable. The soundbite liked to think about that Kevin Costner *Robin Hood* movie in which Denzel Washington is bound to Costner because Costner saved his life. The only way Denzel can be unbound is to reciprocate in life saving. This, thought the soundbite, is love. But the sad fact is that the stalled car will only ever love the train. And my dear soundbite, O soundbite, it's Morgan Freeman in that movie, not Denzel.

WASTOID

My lover is in love with all the checks that have ever been written. He has nicknames for each: 432, 433, etc. Each thing needs unique love, just as a wound needs each piece of shrapnel. But all others from all things draw all that's good. There are so many loves, some shackled & some tattered, some scaled & some bleeding internally. Just today a bomb wounded sixty-two people in a plaza & my lover wrote checks for bills, the mortgage & a donation. My lover loves each check uniquely. But each check speaks the same dialect: a pit-lake laden with arsenic & cadmium. That pit lake is within all who love.

WASTOID

The poet is in bliss because he might die at any moment & he can imagine an object. He can imagine a bereaved widower & an orphaned boy. He can imagine them holding an object. He could have a husband & have a boy & then have an object. The object will never be destroyed by death. Hoarding is a way of squandering. The poet also has an extraneous rib he has not revealed to anyone, but there is not much to say about it, actually.

WASTOID

In the first story the man is chained to a rock & each day he laments. In the second story the man is chained to a rock but he has an enormous Vin Diesel head & each day he rips his torso open with his Vin Diesel teeth & eats his own Vin Diesel liver. In the third story the man is the chain & the rock is the man. In the final story there is no chain & no rock. The man is sitting beside a pool atop a hotel with a nice view of downtown. He is reading a week-old *Wall Street Journal.* The marks on his skin from the frequent burns glow pink in the sunlight. When he dives into the pool, he opens his eyes. Though his eyes sting he sees blurry boys' legs quickly kicking strokes.

WASTOID

My lover is the granting of permanence. He arrives arbitrarily & never when expected. The suffering child becomes eternally suffering while the happy child grows old & sniffs out people-food. The famous are forever happy & misfortunates whistle between two fingers. My lover's secret is that love only lasts if he makes it last. He is giddy with his secret like it is a cache of fancy shampoos. I am a requiem for a forgotten soldier. My theme is haunting but tough to remember. When the clarinets come in the audience weeps, but in the morning each of them pour orange juice out of plastic bottles purchased from Costco, leaving the refrigerator door open while they do.

WASTOID

A belly fell in love with Picasso. But Picasso was already dead. The belly wanted to dig Picasso up & make him love him, but the body the belly was attached to did not understand the belly's desires with such specificity. I have a lot of opinions: I do not think children should attend school; I do not think the Illinois River is the largest & most important water route in the state of Illinois, I think it is the Big Muddy River. The problem with opinions is they become religious or nightmare, e.g., Picasso's Minotaur. But I also love how nightmares fill me, how a river fills a song. Most nightmares are beautiful, though not to the one living them.

Wastoid

My lover is extensive & his definitions are ambiguous.
His crown glows greenly in twilight's whale-light as fields
prick with torture devices. I envy the straightforward art
of catalogs & mortgages, the fat of an octet. I am outcast &
bootless & bridges need bombing & murderers compassion.
Lately delightful memories can't blot lamentations. These
marchers require too many boots outside the Old Country
Buffets, the fatty prime rib.

WASTOID

Lovers have more blood than need. Their blood is always falling out of them & running for state congress. There is a restricted section of the state library for books containing the truth about nature & if the blood wins the election it gains access to this section. Nature can be understood as an encouragement, but what do we do when words are too true? It is unnatural for lovers to keep their blood. Love is a bloodstain. The library doors can never be opened & anyways all the books are merely true. Love kills any image of lovers. They fade. So fade. The bloodstains fade.

WASTOID

Death & love are now just-friends. Love calls some old bros to see what they're up to. They all have babies or Hollywood blockbusters. They all want to reminisce about the old days working champagne bottles into pipe bombs. Love goes for a hike in the mountains & comes across some elk, he approaches them quietly. They don't run away, but they all turn their backs, refusing to pose. Death's bones get better-looking every day—more dust, more chipping, more surveyors steadying their tripods atop them. Death pretends to suffer, self-effaces at his concerts, but this newfound muse-dom makes him feel quite content.

WASTOID

A bald dog fell in love with a cloak. The dog had grown bald from too much petting because he was irresistibly cute. After men pet the hair from him they no longer had a need for him & left him in the woods. The cloak was owned by a very special man who every day wore a brand new cloak, which he never wore again but could not bear to get rid of. His house was full of beautiful cloaks. They pushed at the doors & cracked the storm windows. The day the very special man wore this cloak he met the bald dog during a hike. The very special man rubbed a salve over the bald dog's dry skin, easing the itching. That was when the bald dog fell in love with the cloak. Now the bald dog no longer lives in the forest. Instead he hides beneath the very special man's porch, waiting each day for the very special man to walk out his door simply so that he can sniff the faint smell of his beloved.

WASTOID

My lover is an onlooker & I am a passer-by. If a fight breaks out, if a car wrecks into a diner, if someone spills their yogurt on the president's pants, he is there watching & I am walking by. These days almost anything can draw a crowd around itself, but often people disappear & you wonder what became of them. What happened to Matt? To Andy? To Andy? And Andy? I savor our status as quick-blooming accessories, debris at the bottom of a fountain. The hardware store is burning & for a moment my lover & I make eye contact & I know it has metastasized, love.

WASTOID

My lover has a set of keys that unlock the music that is in me. But I cannot find my lover. Have you seen him? Has he called you or anything? I keep texting him but he hasn't responded. The music is building up in me & it's beginning to feel awkward. Stretch marks have grown where stretch marks should not be. I keep gnawing on all the dead wood I see, trying to make some music out of it. I want to hear that jingling of his key ring. I want to feel the shelter of a correct key sliding into the correct keyhole.

WASTOID

A severed head fell in love with its former body. He thanked the guillotine for bringing them together in this way. He thanked the famished crowd for their need. Some say the skull is the heart, others say it is the flip-phone. The body is so spine & firmament, so closure. Everyone in the crowd simultaneously screamed for blood & posted videos of themselves screaming for blood. Academics are always like *The body, blah, blah, blah,* & they make a good point, but from the basket, resting atop the other severed heads, the severed head blinked twice. His tongue hung from his mouth like a toad. Then his lower lip twitched.

WASTOID

My lover is a collection of tools with indeterminate purposes.
I love him because I love adaptation, fixing, dismantlement,
etc. There is something like a dental pick to him—isn't that
weird? And something else that looks like a cross between a
noose & a saw—what could that be used for? I have no ideas,
no speculation. I am *The Chicago Manual of Style*. I know what
to do. I sing songs so accurate they can't shake an eardrum.
When two brothers walk the old pier, I know to bow when
they slip beneath the gull bones.

Wastoid

I used to bike to these cement rain-gutters in back yards, a between-space where suburban kids in army jackets would smoke ditch-weed & light things on fire & I'd be on an adventure. I didn't imagine things happening—I did not fight any dragons or do spy shit. I was on an adventure. Now I must write all the words I know in chronological order but I'm not sure what to write right now.

WASTOID

My lover is so sincere. When he enters a room, fathers unpop their boys' collars & conceal their comb-overs. Bad art hides from him. Each day is an elaborate eulogy. Everything he does is or deserves an encore. I am an unfinished statue of Atlas, the earth never added to my shoulders. All day & night I strain beneath an intangible burden, my face an unending grimace. Sometimes he comes to look at me, to admire the fine craftsmanship of my pain. He cries more than what would be merely appropriate. He takes notes. He prepares the perfect anecdote for his next speaking engagement & at his next speaking engagement the anecdote is simply perfect.

WASTOID

My lover is a mirage. In the distance when walking in the desert is the only way I see him. Why am I lost in the desert, you might ask. I am a soft drink commercial. It is tedious, but at least it is art. Paintings, pictures, forms, shadows, reflections, perspective—all allude to two in combination. To compliment art is to rub one's own bruised cheek. Love's constructs determine definition how sand grits between my eyelids. Love is limited in how much of a lover it can portray. These bloody cracks in my lips are cinematic, yes, but self-induced.

WASTOID

When my lover turned me into gold, he marveled at my sheen, at my face, so hot in the sun, so cold in the shade. Each night he traced the lines where my arms became my chest. He gave each guest a guided tour of all my precious characteristics. To get me into & out of the house he designed a series of pulleys & as he pulled them he sweated with joy. But then the clouds accumulated & parted, guests came & went. One Sunday morning my lover didn't want to bother with the pulleys & the sweat. Then on a sunny day he kept the curtains closed. When guests came by he put a human mask on me & sat me at the end of the table, telling them I was shy.

WASTOID

I walk through crowds & lay my head on each person's chest, looking for the bosom of my lover. Each chest is like a fresh grave. At the bottom of each grave lies a trinket of nostalgia: a t-ball trophy, a copy of *Playboy*. And so I left the crowds & streetcars for the quiet of the country. But there I found the ground to be an endless series of graves, stretching up mountains past the treeline. With each step I fall into my lover's grave & what with having to climb out of the grave & then falling back into the next one & climbing out & whatnot, I make everything utterly images.

WASTOID

My lover emerged from an abandoned mine, his arms full of rocks covered in writing. It was ancient writing that I could not read, but my lover told me they were poems. He sat beside the mine on a foldout chair & read the poems to me. All of the poems were about my lover. But none of them got him right. One referred to him as a spine, another as a can of used bacon grease. One poem told a story of two bumper cars bumping each other eternally. Another described a well-built house in Lawrence, Massachusetts. But my lover is more than a house, than bumper cars, than a spine. He has a beautiful cheek, no two cheeks. And I owe him twenty dollars.

WASTOID

A confessional fell in love with a priest. All week the confessional anticipated Saturday at five when the priest would hear confessions, anticipated the half-minute or so when the priest would enter the confessional & adjust his chair & silently prepare himself before turning on the green light above the confessional door, this brief time of quiet before sinnermen entered with their guilty Old Spice. The priest, however, was in love with Mark Twain. In the moments before the sinnermen entered he wished he was in the rectory, in the brown chair beside the window, reading Mark Twain. Their relationship seems one-sided & unfair to me, but both of them seem ok with it.

WASTOID

A man made of glass loves a man made of bricks. They know their love is ruinous, so they make, instead of love, comparisons: *Your brick body is like a moon made of bricks; Your glass body is like a steeplechase of glass.* They do this until they run out of true things, & then they invent new true things solely for comparison: *Your brick body is like an engine fueled by David Mamet; Your glass body is like a cul de sac of grape juice.* This went on so long the elements wore the man made of bricks down to brick bones, scuffed the man made of glass to cadaver-skin. They lived on match-heads, lying in the streets, the hot rain melting the sugar from their eyes.

WASTOID

My lover peels numbers from clocks like lips off the mouths of agreeable lovers. He's a famous DJ. I haven't seen him in a decade but I see his face on magazines. When he sees me he sees memory-me but when I see him I see valance. It's DJ Night in America, boys hung by Christmas lights nooses, your spine cemented to keep you upright. Here's a flyer. Take it. There's no date, no time, no RSVP, but there's no cover at the door.

WASTOID

What can't be told can't pass as fantasy but might be love's truth. My copy of Word is registered to Innocent Fantasy, LLC. I buy my coffee from a man with dog eyes. We are lost, lost cases, lost caretakers, & we must go deeper to follow the heart's lead, as if the heart were not a box. Can we allow blue light? Can we do a thing & allow it to make us? We follow a jar into love & the blue light empties outside the office. I want this image in my mind to remain. And this wax imprint of a key. But what unsubtles thought is permission.

Wastoid

A man put his man on one arm of a balancing scale. On the other arm the first man set a pair of cowboy boots. The second man was heavier than the boots & his side of the scale sank. The first man added a party dress but the second man was heavier than the boots & dress. Then the first man removed one of his legs & added it to the scale. Still, the second man was heavier. Then the first man removed his other leg & added it to the scale but the second man was still heavier. Then the first man removed his arms & added them to the scale but the second man was heavier still. Then a cop wandered in & saw the cowboy boots & stepped onto the scale & stole the cowboy boots. This tipped the scale. The cop wandered away. The second man stepped off the scale, picked up the first man's arms & attached them to his own body, just below his own arms. The first man's first set of hands held tightly to his new set of hands.

WASTOID

My lover is six white dudes at an Arbys, hugging while slapping each other's backs, shouting *Yo* then sitting down to curly fries. All matter is made of morsels of matter but when does the accretion distinguish between full moral justification & empty bags of cheetos in the back seat of a car? I am the one-sided mirror through which the psychiatrist watches the patient play. I am only myself when the subject is unaware of my nature. The sign outside, the backlit plastic Arbys sign with the changeable letters that the assistant manager climbs up his ladder to change out by hand, reads *CHICKEN SALAD IS BACK.*

WASTOID

My lover has inter-cooled turbo & when he presses his turbo button human hearts inflame with love & then he is as beautiful as a billboard. When a man happens by he sees the inter-cooled turbo & caresses my lover. The turbo causes a body of water to heat & create a steamy bath in which men immerse themselves to cure illnesses. But I wish my lover was a column of fire & his turbo a hotter fire within fire, as hot as a jackal's eyes, so hot the hymnals drip from the pews. I am so sick with love for my lover that there is no fire or water & animals fall dead with swollen tongues emerging from their mouths. If only the turbo could truly be cooled. If only I could see through the jackal's eyes.

WASTOID

My lover is the largest bubblegum bubble. He extends beyond the reaches of the solar system. Past hail, zero gravity & comets he perseveres. He is ever-expanding. It is really pretty inspirational, his journey. I am the single breath that forever blows to expand the bubble of my lover, forever creating him with my self's excess. A breath can be a pharmaceutical state, but etymology teaches that no bubble lasts forever. At the buffet line after the funeral I know I will be the one who grabs with my fingers the piece of cantaloupe with the serving fork attached to it.

WASTOID

My lover is the goal of the wrestling match. When I look at him one way I am certain he is *To Win*. He has that spiky look, as if he just got out of the salon. But at other times he looks like *To Understand*—he has a wise beard & there are always windows behind him & the windows behind him are always flooded with light. At these points I address him in decorous phrasing, for I am the blood that dissolves salt. I am the sad slave of healing. I turn the radio dial until the car falls off the bridge & I don't even care if there is water down there.

WASTOID

My lover is a scoreboard. He values freedom & every time he turns around it is another season. After a game completes he does not remember it. Memory makes a paparazzi light— everyone is equal in the highlight reel. I am a character, the antagonist, hanging from the edge of a tall building. The hero has the option of saving me or letting me fall. I am screaming & begging him: *You're not like me. You can't just let me die.* The audience knows the hero will save me but savor the hope he won't, that he'll let narrative escape control. Close up on my fingers slipping in increments. Close up on the look in my eyes. Silence the soundtrack to only my rough breath. If no one loses it's not a game.

WASTOID

My lover's real story is in exports. He is polluted beyond use. He is sinking slowly into himself. Clearly there is much more unpaved than paved land but the fabled Atlantis was based on a real city & five years ago Coca Cola did not even exist. I mean, we can't define what *beyond use* means. Or perhaps what I really mean is when my lover sneezes he sounds just like my father. You don't even have to do anything to be a good person these days.

WASTOID

My lover rents my love out by the hour. Men book my love &
during their hour they are in love how I am in love with my
lover: like handful of caraway seeds, like a moon evermore
three-quarters full. When no clients have booked my love
it returns to me, abrupt & cruel, at the top of the hour as
I stand on a pier, sit at a diner. Love can be propaganda,
a sonata over-practiced into prickliness. But to be in love
one must always climb higher on the mountain. But when
I climb that high I exclude so much of the world & what
is excluded itself I find most lovable. I would have been so
unhappy as Mr. Nineteenth Century.

WASTOID

My lover is a vacant church. I am the nearly empty gas tank inside a city bus. We have so much in common that we are unable to see one another, passing like cadavers under streetlights, dancing in each other's arms but noting nothing but the dancing. I want to be filled & to fill him with the organ's shriek, but only hope fills a vacant church. I want to play that song that rests with the lamb & rises with the lark, but instead I am making obligation. If one pulls the cord the bus will stop & I don't even care. I want vacancy, not this perpetual loom. Where there is a window I want there to be a door. I cannot be an organ, nor an organist.

WASTOID

My lover is a paper airplane a boy let fly inside the Guggenheim. The child made my lover out of a brochure & folding. My lover lies with faith. Air will always support him. This panorama will always pan. The Guggenheim will exist forever & my lover will always be mid-air. It is like a father nursing a child who seems to be asleep, or the end of *Hamlet*: there are lovers & there are those in love. But I am out of cash & the strip on my card has lost its spirit. The ATM screen tells me *Press enter to exit.* I must enter to exit.

Wastoid

My lover has a body of ashes. He sits in a windowless room
& tries not to move. When I am with him I must hold my
breath & sweat layers my arms. He is so still, he is a zoo of
stillness & all of the animals are ferocious. I am a labyrinth
of faces, each holding its breath, each turning blue, talking
to & answering itself without breath. Christ, I am tired. I am
all the colors in a painting of the moon.

WASTOID

My beloved is an extravagant figure of speech. He hints at visions & notions beyond language's right to describe. He impresses people. When he stands by a fir tree people circle the tree holding hands, whispering facts into the needles. When he holds hands with someone invisible that person becomes a cake bought from a real bakery. When a sad person nears him the sad person blooms into an unstoppable ladder. I am the shadow of an enormous outdoor Miro sculpture, my lines tweaked ragged by the shaggy grass. I circle my sculpture by day & then withdraw at night. If my beloved stood within me I would become a ream of paper or anything soakable with lighter fluid & wakable with fire.

Wastoid

I fell in love with my sight. My sight may grant a thousand errors but each proves his presence. On nights when all I can do is stand beside a friend as he talks to someone else & then move on to stand beside another friend & so on, I reach my hand below my eyes & my sight holds me & there is nothing that cannot be downloaded somewhere. When night silts my sight is there to guide me into the back seat of its Subaru in the graveyard where the tombstones have epitaphs with fill-in-the-blanks. The word *sin* means rejection. The word *sin* means untouched. Even marvelous things can be effortlessly forgotten.

WASTOID

A neutered dog fell in love with another neutered dog. They chased each other across the dusty dogpark. Their black spots got hot from the sun. They have an address for a rooming house, but they cannot find it. The guy at the gas station does not know where it is. The guy at the 7-11 has never heard of this rooming house. The two dogs had been told that each room has its own private bathroom. They hope to find this rooming house. They hope to stay a while.

Wastoid

My lover is a surprising accent. When the jury chairman says *moity* for *mighty*, when you find yourself hitting the hard vowels extra firmly, when the stranger's southern accent emerges after his third drink, my lover is there. Though one might ask *What does your crystal mean?* & another *Who's Will?* there is always meat cut from the cow, always buzz in a recording. I am a glass replica of a body designed for anatomical study. My coat of arms is a plain design of two fields, one white & one black, flanked on either side by the words *No*. When I move my mouth to make meaning dust puffs out. When my glass throat cracks I'll be long gone for the freight trains. I'll be huddled around the word *lonely*. But for now, I'm not unlike you, ancestral.

WASTOID

A gameshow's cheering was in love with a three-load capacity washing machine that spun clothes into an incorruptible blur. The washing machine had many lovely fuckbuddies & this gave the gameshow's cheering hope— despairing hope, but hope. Then the washing machine fell in love with a dryer, an older model with a bit of gum stuck inside. One night over drinks the washing machine told the gameshow's cheering what he really loved was the ease: *It's so easy. I wash the clothes & he dries them. It's so easy. It's like holding an axe.* Despite this the gameshow's cheering's hope would not go away. It hung around the house like a holiness. It ordered pizza topped with pineapple, knowing full well the gameshow's cheering hated nothing so much as pineapple pizza. And through all of this the gameshow's cheering could express his sadness only through cheering.

WASTOID

There are four kinds of love, each with meaning:

    Antimony: I must attend time's leisure.

    Love: Sometimes there is meat, moan.

    Cholera: Be cautious & consider what a play-actor means.

    Dairy Queen: Dairy Queen.

WASTOID

My lover is real rain asking abstract rain for renewal. He is
the wist of standing in the rain, the astonishing dullness of
rain, the take-my-hand of rain. There is no summer. There
is no ice. There is only what emerges from a taped-up box.
I'm the intern with the bad shoes. The same day wakes me
from every nap. I want to capture the impossibility of my
lover & paint it on my face. I want to paint my face like a
panda.

WASTOID

My lover is a 911 call. At night the outlets leak electricity onto the hardwood floor & I lick at it. I want everything emergency, the frantic phrasing, the rapid breath uncalmable by an operator's calm. The first time I saw a dead man I was ten. He lay beside the train tracks & what I remember most was he had no shoes on & his socks were very dirty & I still wanted to leave my pennies on the train tracks but I did not leave pennies on the train tracks. I step in front of speeding trucks. I walk with my feet on the roof's edge. Out on the ice one cannot know if the ice is moving.

WASTOID

My lover is a pair of balls dangling beneath a kilt. He is a preparation for absence, a message always either being written or read. The way he slips on a hot summer night embassies between body & a copy of *La Vita Nuova* checked out of a high school library & never returned. I see white men with dreads. I see Northern Virginia whites noodle-dancing in bridal shalwar kameezs. Everywhere the smell of nag champa & tea tree oil. Everything buoyed by the synth patch in "Purple Rain." My lover is carried off by a foreign crowd, dangling in flower petals & howling, the absence finally clearly the absence between an urn & a vessel.

WASTOID

My lover is nostalgia for the misdeeds of youth. He is drinking alone while the blur tvs. It's difficult to remember pain but it's more difficult to remember before pain. We make our love how we make mucus to fill tired lungs. I am of fortunate birth, a set of clothes one purchases for a new job. All my buildings are built of windows—even my dirt gets shipped in. Take all comfort in worth & truth, take the deserted street hanging from the windows of the bus, take what pauses you to you. I am despised by shadow, crowned in race: details change, scars fade.

WASTOID

My beloved is all-the-lights & I want to be all-the-lights but I am a laminated press-pass. I once loved a crack in the asphalt but nothing grew out of him. When he died there was so much broken glass of every imaginable color & I made a kiln out of it & I stood too close to the kiln & the heat made my laminate grow cloudy & now it is very difficut to read me. When I think of all-the-lights I think of how dark things must seem to be him, how when one is all-the-lights all else is darkness. What darkness makes of me, I will never understand. In darkness I am the cover of a magazine.

Wastoid

The word yearn is descended from a small rodent-like creature that lived off the eggs of superb birds. We yearn so hard into art that it only makes more art. A lover's life's concerto can be studied from the perspective of any number of impediments, but google it all night long & you won't be any closer to the steps of Pandemonium.

WASTOID

I drink my milk from the corner of the paper carton & return the empty carton to the fridge. I was born on Saturn, or somewhere near Saturn. I am in love with a man who was born on Saturn. When he raises his hand to a chattering crowd they silence. In his youth his speech about death won him an award. When you die the people who love you get very, very sleepy. Once I shut my eyes tight & they stayed shut. Once one enters the labyrinth there is no means of escape. The substance has been sucked out & only accidents remain. You are getting sleepy, sleepy, & then you are asleep.

Wastoid

My lover is the anonymous tip that will send an innocent man to the electric chair. He lives alone in the desert. He avoids anyone who could contact police. At night he ties his mouth closed with a green bandana. This is earthquake weather, a rolodex of dust, & no one answers for family. This is dying with the inability to make similes. I am a ring that fell off the victim's hand in the back seat of the car before his carcass was weighted & dropped in the pond. Muck accumulates & the body decomposes but I wait for someone with good eyes to find me. My lover's silence is my lover's skin, such innocence unused at pondbottom.

WASTOID

My lover is a crossroads I must always return to. I am a boy
made of honey. I live in an old gas station & keep the air
conditioner on. Each time I return to the crossroads I roll
the dice & gamble with the juke-joint epiphaniphiliacs. I
always win but I always cheat. There are so many endings to
the game: the vanishing dude, the lost lover in the storm. My
lover impatiently awaits my endless returns, half-buffered &
shaking hands with the suffering sun. Behind me my honey-
trail attracts small ants who get eaten by large ants who get
eaten by larger ants & so on & so on until it's an encyclopedia.

WASTOID

An I fell in love with what is beneath the rock. But when one picks the rock up what was beneath the rock is no longer what is beneath it & depending on where & how you hold the rock you might even be beneath it. An I never tires of relation's fiasco, its eternal chambers of cinder. From the I's point of view it looked like what is beneath the rock is actually a little cloud. *Are you a little cloud?* he asked. *I fear that I am not like you. For I walk through the aisles of grocery stores & smell the cut flowers but I never buy them. I hear warbling birds but I don't feed them.* When a body dies the I never existed. All the while what is beneath the rock continues until a hot fire explodes it—& even then, though, isn't there more to understand?

WASTOID

What I left in love was never mine, a winter coat I shed from fear, a chunk of yellowcake kept as souvenir. I let my four tongues grow slack. I trip as I walk the dark trail. Sometimes writing poems is easy & sometimes it is complicated & neither ensures a good poem. After your lover leaves & you are still in love with him & he is still in love with you a settling occurs. The leaves, they get magnificent. The piled pills, split moons & gel-caps, rebel. Blankness becomes hope & what is hoped, glue. There is a blankness in each solitary bed, that's where love sleeps.

WASTOID

My lover owns a tire store. He is powerful & therefore he is cruel. He has many expensive pieces of jewelry & he wears all of them all of the time. His neck is so buried in necklaces that only his eyes peek over the jewels & gold. Someone has built a large wooden box in the tire store & filled it with sawdust & corn meal & is raising mealworms in it. My lover cannot see the box because his jewelry blocks his vision, but the musty odor of the mealworms reaches him. He thinks he should find this odor objectionable, but it reminds him of when he lived in a rotting home & each night rot lulled him to sleep. His throat was so bare then, all the tires flammable.

WASTOID

I can't remember why but my lover walked home carrying his shoes.

WASTOID

You're born, you spend your life trying to understand, &
then, is that so sad? Who's to tell the child to stop salting
the slug? Think of Marvin Gaye's *Midnight Love*: I had only
ever listened to "Sexual Healing" & then one day listened
to the whole thing—demented pillow talk over ominous
Gary Numan synth-bass, angular jazz chords played on
an expressionless harpsichord patch & then in the middle,
Marvin's aviary of a voice, which really does make it worse.
It's enough to make the steps stop. It's like one day you take
the mask off & look at the city & the city is a city of militias,
lovers armed & marching in formation, the buildings not
even burning, bodies not even piled up in the parks, & is
that even sad?

WASTOID

Approaching home fell in love with walking in the front door. Walking in the front door couldn't love approaching home—he reminded him of what could be. Approaching home loved walking in the front door & wanted to be him. When walking in the front door posted a clip from *How I Met Your Father* on facebook approaching home bought the whole season with two-day shipping. It is hard to love, to first acknowledge the crumpled man beside the road & then slow one's car & then stop one's car, then exit the car & walk toward the crumpled man & bend down toward the crumpled man & touch his rigid, shivering hands.

WASTOID

I have this game called *Tell*. No one taught me the rules & it is like trying to play a game after only having seen a picture of people playing the game. In my lover I wander from room to room & sit down & feel all the feelings & feel how those feelings feel & then I find someone to tell what I feel. Sometimes it's Rat Park in DC in the 90s. Sometimes it's the dude who works at Denny's. The only game I know is *Don't*. It is an easy game, but to win one must step off a downtown parking garage & I don't want to want to win.

WASTOID

Every time there is one person there are four people. When one dies, the other three take the one apart & search for the tiny steel statue of the saint. When a person falls in love with themselves they cut themselves open in search of the tiny steel statue of the saint. Rarely do they find it before all the blood comes out. My lover contains the tiny steel statue of the saint. But unbeknownst to him, the statue has grown enormous & has replaced every part of his body. Only steel now remains beneath his skin & he is saintly in his immobility, the steel face impelling his skin face into a new face & I must love even this face.

WASTOID

Now I recognize everyone I have ever seen. For instance, on the walk over here I heard two men discussing how hot one of them was one night—the one man thought the other was very hot but the hot-that-night man didn't think he was at his hottest. I saw one man walking while holding a guitar & singing out of tune. I saw one man with long pant legs. I saw sky behind the men & stars behind the sky & if I were to close my eyes there'd be nothing in front of me, a chasm awaiting my foot, & I'd fall into the eternal ball-pit of the Chuck E Cheese & all the employees on fire, neverdying. Medicine works that way: for me, like love, it is faith. And when I think of my lover there is fire & when I put my hand over him I burn.

WASTOID

Truth has two natures. One the one we think of as nature: trees, bears, all that shit. The other a song so dutiful that the DJ can call it a hit with his mouth sewn shut. This is why love is inevitable. Everyone makes out with everyone beneath the canopy. But there is misery to each station ID & the between-song bathos. Dead air dangles like a hockey mask & then the opening riff to "Senator's Son" arrives & love is secure for a few days more. We must all hope, though, that there's somewhere out there a bridge that wants to collapse, a nineteen-year-old opening a DuChamp book for the first time, & if you position yourself just so beside the escalators the pedestrians really are all headless.

Wastoid

My lover is toil & to learn each must have him at some point. We must work on the assembly line for five years & feel my lover & then spend forty-five years writing about that feeling. We retell the story of the box of rotten flounder until somebody announces we exist. I am a somber mood—people rarely seek me out. I have the body of a shadow & also the soul of a shadow. But while I compound as the many streetlights cast me in multiplicities, my lover ages from iron into flesh: tales of toil told later grow more port-of-origin. I bivouac in Delaware. I refuge in Ohio. All that remains are jewels.

WASTOID

I put my face on his face & bam!, no more face. Even when faced with my lover telling day & night how fortunate they are, writing sonnets of absolute devotion is a brutal headbutt. I put my hand to my lover's hand & our hands are buried in clover. I peek & my lover peeks & we are buried in clover. Absence continues, everywhere identical. To find what makes evening so bright look first & then find.

WASTOID

Love is a silence following silence into creeks of venomous snakes. He takes the radio apart & leaves the pieces on the stairs. He spends the bag of silver dollars on candy. All the cars have antennas that rise so high. All the pianos stutter. A story of life breaks in chewed nostalgia. Love is a memory of a mirror. Love is a list. For the boys who died before they were born. The boys who died of my love. The boys with names conjured but unapplied: Wolfgang, Wolfgang, Wolfgang to the pyre, Wolfgang to the brittle snakebite of night, soft as dust, dead as dreams.

WASTOID

Love is a non sequitur. I start off loving knock-knock jokes & then I merely love the knocking. I pull into the left lane to pass the Toyota & the Toyota accelerates & I pull back behind it & the Toyota again slows down. From my apartment's open window I hear someone scream *Oh God! No!* & I can't tell if they're joking. It is a lonely road, the road to love, but masses of ants swarm between the sidewalk stones. If you travel long enough on this road you'll run into someone you know.

Wastoid

My eyes & my heart used to simply pass in the hall to the laundry room & nod, each thinking what a dick the other is. But now my eyes push folded papers beneath my heart's door & when my heart unfolds them the papers say *You suck* or *Go back where you came from.* My heart came from the same place as my eyes, but they are made of different stuff. I want to know the problem but my problem is in understanding. For instance, in this jpeg of a photo of Harry Tompkins atop a horse, the look on his face is inscrutable. He is looking up & to the right—it is as if there is something he is about to know, but we can't know this knowledge. There should be a word for this expression & I should be able to recognize this word in the expression. I know his heart would have been in his chest when he was alive & his eyes in the hollows of his skull, but in an image what lies beneath skin? I want to know what they put in the dirt that makes it so raw, but each time I press zoom his face pixelates.

Wastoid

My lover puts his jacket on & zips it to the top. His voice is impossibly reliable. Now we go back to Chicago & he says he needs to get the beautiful water & so he drives thirty miles, forty miles & goes there every time to get the water. I order the banana split because it is the most expensive item on the menu. There's a rebirth hiding somewhere: argyle on the chests of broken-finger boys. It gets cold. It gets hot. Things are & then they were. Now my lover is thirty, he's thirty-seven, & he gets off the bus.

WASTOID

Some nights some stars flutter to earth with the leaves. The leaves burn up instantly but in that instant they are in love. I thumb through an old *GQ* calendar of hot men with brown hair & I think about how lovely is the light that strikes the pages. I am something someone slips beneath my door. Then someone slips something beneath my door & I am in love with myself: a green-starred sleeve over black eyes, a toy car the color of a mountain, coming together to fall apart. I am real because the well is real.

WASTOID

My lover is a whole heap of little horses. He would make me sad if he didn't make me so sleepy. In love, everything must go. It's a fire sale, a salt mine, a Toyotathon. Quietly we slip down this complete cliff of anticipation/terror & all those little horses bounce on each rock as a single heap & grunt in unison. At night my lover comes to me & enters me & just like that, I am asleep. O capital-L Love, of heavy wind, of cathedral sprung full-formed from the face of the cliff: you wearied us home in your hairless arms then left us alone in the night. What the night does not know is that there are thousands of job listings on Craigslist, if he could only get past the dick-pics & dreams.

WASTOID

Love like moss & buttermilk. Love like a stepstool that has never been cleaned. Lover, here's your tent & sleeping bag. Lover, let me hand feed you your pills. The bridge blots the stars but we must assume there are still stars. We must assume so many things. The man with the feather in his hair takes out the recycling. The man with the quirky socks asks his father for money for the gumball machine. Skeeball. Dig-Dug. Spondee. Worrywart. Love wants a clear view with margins. Love wants a fresh trail. Lover, I can see your tag, the tongue cut from the cow's mouth continues to twitch. O my lover, cunning lover, feeble lover, do not fear, fire cannot burn you.

Acknowledgments

This book is indebted to Sara Renee Marshall, Zachary Schomburg, Danielle Vogel, Alisa Heinzman, Joshua Marie Wilkinson, Renee Gladman, Julia Cohen, Dave Carillo, Teal Gardner, Noah Eli Gordon, Sommer Browning, Cassandra Smith, Oren Silverman, Robert Cataldo, J. Michael Martinez, Seth Landman, Dan Singer, Jennifer Denrow, Heather Streckfus-Green, Elisabeth Reinkordt, Julie Carr, Karla Kelsey, Helene Cixous, William Shakespeare, Selah Saterstrom & all those who love those with neck tattoos.

Pieces of this book have appeared in *Word Riot*, *Timber*, *Diode*, *The Fanzine*, *Notnostrums*, *Ampersand*, *Sixth Finch*, *Fruita Pulp*, *Fourteen Hills*, *The Colorado Review*, *Houseguest*, *Puerto del Sol*, *Toad*, *Big Lucks*, *New Orleans Review*, *Zero Ducats*, in the SP CE Gallery *LUV POEMZ* anthology & in *The Sonnets*, edited by Paul Legault & Sharmila Cohen. Jenifer Park designed & printed a beautiful broadside of the Arby's one.

Thanks to editors Nicolle Elizabeth, Alexis Almeida, Ella Longpre, Luke Bloomfield, Corey Zeller, Kyle Harvey, Rob MacDonald, Roberto Montes, Paul French, Lisa Summe, Scott Schwalenberg, Sasha Steensen, Scott Alexander Jones, Ryan Nash, Patty Paine, Mark Yakich, & to all who devote time to literary stuff.

This book's title was inspired by Wasteoid, a metal band from Lincoln, Nebraska. Jeff from Wasteoid died during the time I was writing this book. He was loved & he is missed.